DANCE

Dance TEAM

by Wendy Garofoli

Consultant:
Sara Haley
Dance Team Choreographer and Consultant

press ®

Mankato, Minnesota

Snap Books are published by Capstone Press,
151 Good Counsel Drive, P.O. Box 669, Mankato, Minnesota 56002.
www.capstonepress.com

Library of Congress Cataloging-in-Publication Data

Garofoli, Wendy.
    Dance Team / Wendy Garofoli.
    p. cm.—(Snap books. Dance)
    Summary: "Describes dance team, including training, moves, and
competition"—Provided by publisher.
    Includes bibliographical references and index.
    ISBN-13: 978-1-4296-0120-7 (hardcover)
    ISBN-10: 1-4296-0120-5 (hardcover)
    1. Dance—Juvenile literature. 2. Dance Teams—Juvenile literature.
I. Title. II. Series.
GV1798.G37 2008
792.8—dc22
                                           2006102782

Editor: Becky Viaene

Designer: Veronica Bianchini

Photo Researchers: Charlene Deyle and Wanda Winch

Photo Credits:
AP/Wide World Photos/Bizuayehu Tesfaye, 28; Capstone Press/Karon Dubke, all except pages 28, 29, and 32; Courtesy
of the author Wendy Garofoli, 32; The Image Works/Topham, 29

Capstone Press would like to thank the Gustavus Adolphus College Dance Team in Saint Peter, Minnesota, for their
assistance with this book.

Table of Contents

Chapter 1
Dancing Together 4

Chapter 2
Training for Tryouts 6

Chapter 3
Dancing Machine 12

Chapter 4
T is For Team 26

Glossary 30

Fast Facts 30

Read More 31

Internet Sites 31

About the Author 32

Index 32

Chapter One

DANCING TOGETHER

Do you enjoy being part of a team and have a passion for dancing?

Then get ready to bust some moves. Combine your creativity and coordination by joining a great group—a dance team.

Dance teams are known for their ability to perform the same moves at the same time with amazing precision. Even with about 20 dancers, everyone's moves are sharp and together.

You can try out for your school dance team. Many dance studios and cheerleading gyms also have dance teams that train for competitions. Some of the best dancers make it on professional dance teams or dance lines, like the Laker Girls and the Radio City Rockettes.

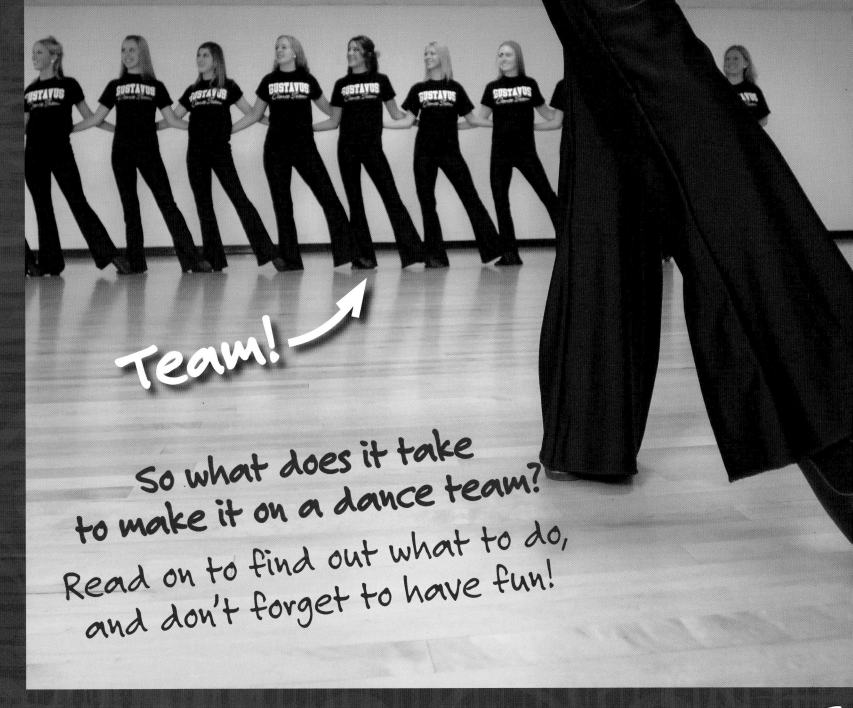

Team!

So what does it take to make it on a dance team? Read on to find out what to do, and don't forget to have fun!

Chapter Two

TRAINING FOR TRYOUTS

Do you want to try out for the dance team, but you don't know where to start?

You can improve your chances of making it on the team by taking dance lessons before tryouts. Beginner ballet, jazz, or hip-hop dance classes are your best bet. Work hard and have a positive attitude at tryouts, and you can make it on the team.

A lot of the questions I get are about getting ready for tryouts. The best advice I can give is to take a dance class. Years of training are important but it's always good to take a class to sharpen up the skills.

—Christine Zoffinger, dance team head coach for Rutgers University

Flexibility

You can start getting ready for tryouts by stretching to improve your flexibility. Try sitting with your legs split, with one to each side. Stretch by leaning toward each leg for a few seconds. Finally, reach forward and try to touch your stomach to the ground while keeping your legs straight.

Ready to kick it up a level? Before you start kicking or jumping, remember to stretch your lower leg muscles. Stand with your arms straight out in front of you and your hands on a wall. Step one leg back and bend your other leg toward the wall. Lean toward the wall and you'll feel the stretch in your straight leg.

Strength

To be a dance team member, you'll need to be strong. Push-ups and sit-ups are great ways to build stomach and back strength.

For push-ups, lie on your stomach. Put your palms on the floor about shoulder length apart. Push your arms straight up. Bend your elbows and then straighten them. See how many push-ups you can do!

Start sit-ups by lying on your back with your knees bent and feet flat on the floor. Put your arms straight out by your sides or cross them over your chest. Then lift up toward your knees.

Finally, get active. Running, jumping rope, or doing anything that gets your heart rate up will prepare you for a fast-paced dance team tryout.

Making Tryouts Terrific

Remember all the practicing and stretching you did to prepare for dance team tryouts? When tryout day finally arrives, it's time to put that training to good use.

Tryouts are your chance to really shine. Combine the right moves with a positive attitude and you'll give a winning performance.

Most dance team tryouts begin with a coach teaching everyone a short dance routine. Later, you'll perform the routine in front of judges in a small group or alone. The judges will be watching you from the minute you walk through the door. Wow them with your energy, great technique, eye contact, and personality.

You may make a few mistakes, but that doesn't mean you won't make the team. If you do make a mistake, act confident and keep dancing. And no matter what, don't stop smiling.

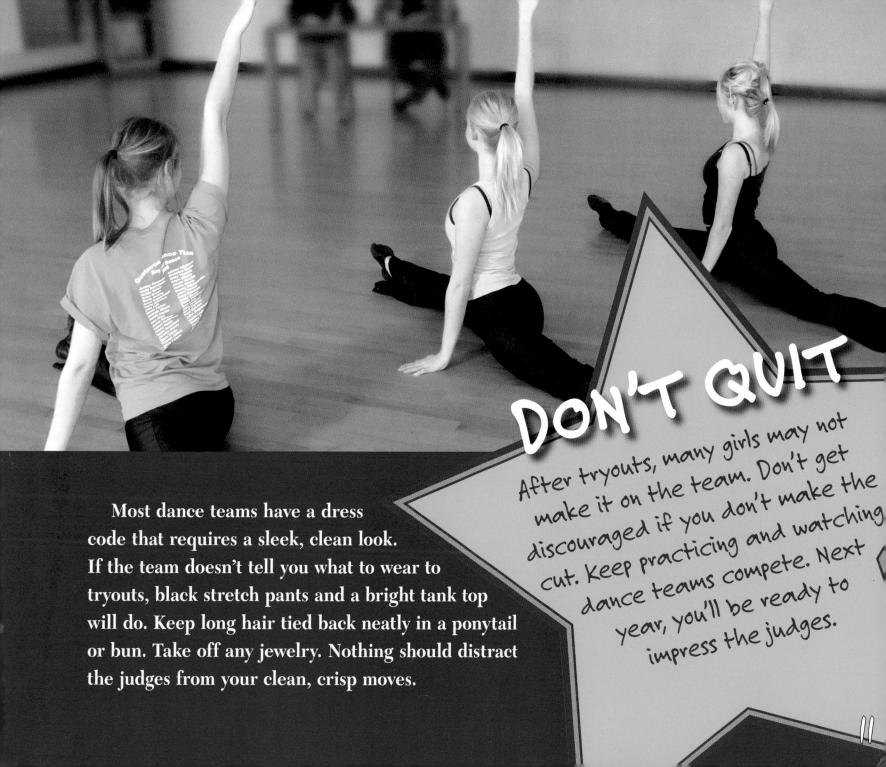

Most dance teams have a dress code that requires a sleek, clean look. If the team doesn't tell you what to wear to tryouts, black stretch pants and a bright tank top will do. Keep long hair tied back neatly in a ponytail or bun. Take off any jewelry. Nothing should distract the judges from your clean, crisp moves.

DON'T QUIT

After tryouts, many girls may not make it on the team. Don't get discouraged if you don't make the cut. Keep practicing and watching dance teams compete. Next year, you'll be ready to impress the judges.

Chapter Three

DANCING MACHINE

So what steps can you expect to perform once you've made it on the dance team? You'll likely be learning three styles of dance: jazz, pom, and hip-hop.

Jazz

Jazz has been performed since the 1920s. But it's only been popular with dance teams since the late '80s. Jazz has helped dance teams become better dancers and use more difficult moves in their routines.

Dance teams perform different kinds of jazz dance. There's lyrical jazz, which is soft and similar to ballet. Street jazz borrows some moves from hip-hop. There's even something called thrashy jazz, which is very rock 'n' roll. Regardless of the style performed, dance team jazz must be danced clean and perfectly together.

Perfect Pirouettes

Three popular steps are used in most dance team jazz routines. The first one is called a pirouette. To do a pirouette a dancer places one foot on the side or in front of her opposite knee. Then she turns around in place on the other leg. Pirouettes are difficult and require excellent balance. When dancers get very good, they can turn three, four, or even five times around. Now imagine a whole team doing that together!

balance!

Crazy about Kicking

The second jazz step you'll often use is a high kick called a grand battement. To do this step, kick up one leg toward your shoulder and point your toes. Keep your back and other leg straight while you kick.

Some dance teams do grand battements while linking arms in a straight line. This is called a kickline. Some teams even create an entire routine with just kicks.

grand battement!

15

Love to Leap?

Practicing a dance team jazz routine can be exciting and challenging. The final, and most difficult, jazz step you'll use will have you leaping—literally.

jeté!

This step is called a jeté, or split leap. You step off one foot and split your legs in the air. Then you land back on the ground with the other foot. In order to leap, you'll need strength and flexibility.

Don't get frustrated if you can't master these jazz moves right away. They take lots of practice and flexibility. Even the best dancers keep working to perfect them.

Pretty with Pom

In 1930, people curiously waited to see the first dance drill team perform. This team's style was a lot like cheerleader dances—sharp arm movements accented with pom-pons.

friends!

Today, pom-pons are used in dance team competitions. For performances, pom-pons are usually only used by some teams during basketball and football games. But dance teams still continue to use those crisp arm moves. This style of dance is known as pom.

One of the most important parts of pom are your hands. Place them in fists or flat and straight in blades. Then get ready to move those arms.

V and T

The high and low "V" are base moves of pom. Your arms will be in a "V" shape—either raised above your shoulders or placed low by your hips. Make sure you keep your arms slightly in front of you and your shoulders pressed down.

"T" and half "T" are the other base moves of pom. A "T" movement is when your arms are in a straight line at your shoulders. When you bend your arms in at the elbow, that's called a half "T."

Toe Touches

More advanced pom dancers do toe touches. Start with your feet together and bend your knees to help push you off the floor. Then jump up in the air.

Split your legs in a straddle, so that they make a "V" along with your arms. Land back in the starting position, with your knees bent.

Patterns with Pom

A very good pom routine uses different levels. Team members sit, kneel, bend, and stand to create pretty displays. Pom is all about making interesting patterns and formations as you dance.

Hip-hop: Don't Stop

The first hip-hop dancers began making up their moves in the early 1970s. The original elements of hip-hop dance include popping, locking, and breaking. Today, many dance teams blend those old elements into routines.

Some dance teams also include new hip-hop styles. A popular new style is called krumping. Krumping is a mix of quick, jerky moves. You've probably seen this type of dance in music videos.

Popping and Locking

Many dance teams use popping and locking in their routines. These styles require tons of practice and patience, but they'll definetly get a crowd's attention.

Popping combines smooth moves with the tensing of certain muscle groups. Dancers tense, or pop, their muscles for a few seconds. Then they relax the muscles. Teams often pop their arms, legs, or chests.

Locking is all about big, exaggerated moves, like circling your arms and pointing. When dancers hit their poses, it looks like their bodies are locked into place.

Breaking

The most famous and eye-catching
hip-hop dance style is breaking. Dance teams often
use breaking power moves such as shoulder freezes. For a
shoulder freeze, a dancer rests her head and one shoulder on
the ground. Then she kicks her legs in the air. To make the
move harder, she can place her hands on the ground.

K-kicks are another popular move. Dancers start by doing
a one-handed handstand. Then they quickly twist their body
forward and open their legs overhead.

All about Attitude

Remember two important things when learning hip-hop: Get low and get loose! Hip-hop is danced low to the ground. So you should be bending your knees almost all the time. Try to forget your nice posture you used in those high kicks. You need to be able to move your rib cage, shoulders, and hips. Most importantly, hip-hop is all about attitude! When you're dancing, let your personality shine.

25

Chapter Four

T IS FOR TEAM

After learning all of those dance moves, how can your dance team make them look unified and precise? Practice, practice, practice! You can count on spending a lot of time and energy getting those steps right. Sometimes your dance team will spend a whole practice drilling and working on just a couple of moves. Drilling takes patience and hard work from the entire team.

When you are drilling, one person can stand outside of the group to watch for any mistakes and make corrections. Usually, that person is the coach. Most teams also have captains, who are senior team members who work to make the team its best. It's important to listen to your coach and captains and respect their decisions. The more you prove yourself to be a team player, the better chance you have of becoming a captain some day.

27

Ready to Rock It

With lots of hard work, your team will soon be ready to perform at competitions. Many national dance team competitions are held each year throughout the United States. Your team could even become national champions one day!

And the fun doesn't have to stop once you've graduated from high school or college. You could continue your dance career by becoming a dance team instructor. You also could use your skills to become part of a professional dance team.

Radio City!

Once you turn 18, you can audition to be part of the world famous Radio City Rockettes. But be prepared, competition is fierce. Only the best of the best make it on this team.

One day, dance team competition may be an event that's added to the Olympics. But no matter what dance team you join, always remember the secret to success is working together!

Glossary

drill (DRIL)—to practice dance moves over and over

grand battement (GRAND BAT-munt)—a dance move where one leg is straightened and kicked forward, to the side, or behind

pirouette (puhr-uh-WET)—a complete turn of the body on one foot; pirouettes are commonly used in jazz dancing.

toe touch (TOH TUHCH)—a straddle leap that starts and ends with both feet together and knees bent

Fast Facts

The exact origins of dance teams are unclear. Some say they sprang from marching band drill teams. Others believe that dance teams are based off of cheerleading.

During some performances, the Radio City Rockettes have only 80 seconds to change costumes.

Some dance teams use handbags, hats, chairs, and wigs as props.

Professional dance teams may have up to 50 different costumes.

Read More

Adoue-Johansen, Summer. *The Ultimate Guide to Dance Team Tryout Secrets (Jr./Sr. High).* Bossier City, La.: Darnell Spirit Productions, 2003.

Coachman, Mary Kaye. *Dance Team.* Team Spirit! New York: Rosen, 2007.

Valliant, Doris. *Dance Teams.* Let's Go Team: Cheer, Dance, March. Philadelphia: Mason Crest, 2003.

Internet Sites

FactHound offers a safe, fun way to find Internet sites related to this book. All of the sites on FactHound have been researched by our staff.

Here's how:

1. Visit *www.facthound.com*

2. Choose your grade level.

3. Type in this book ID **1429601205** for age-appropriate sites. You may also browse subjects by clicking on letters, or by clicking on pictures and words.

4. Click on the **Fetch It** button.

Facthound will fetch the best sites for you!

About the Author

Wendy Garofoli is a writer for several magazines, including *Dance Spirit*, *Dance Teacher*, *Pointe*, and *Cheer Biz News*. She was a member of the New York University (NYU) Purple & White Dance Team for four years, two of which she served as captain. In her senior year, the team won the national championship at National Dance Alliance's Collegiate Competition. She went on to coach Columbia University's dance team for three years, and continues to choreograph for various dance teams.

Index

breaking, 22, 24

competitions, 4, 18, 28, 29

dance lessons, 6
dance styles,
    hip-hop, 6, 12, 22–25
    jazz, 6, 12–16
    pom, 12, 18–21
dress code, 11
drilling, 26

exercise, 8–9

flexibility, 8, 16

grand battement, 15

high kick. See grand battement

jeté, 16

k-kicks, 24
krumping, 22

locking, 22, 23

pirouettes, 14
popping, 22, 23
professional dance teams, 4, 28, 29

Radio City Rockettes, 4, 29

shoulder freezes, 24
split leap. See jeté
strength, 9, 16

toe touches, 20
tryouts, 6, 8, 9, 10, 11